Simple Estate and Asset Planning   Jon A. Zahaby, Esq.

Simple Estate and Asset Planning: A Guide to Protect Your Family's Future

by

Jon A. Zahaby, Esq.

Simple Estate and Asset Planning:
A Guide to Protect Your Family's Future

This book is a comprehensive guide to estate and asset planning that offers readers practical advice on how to protect their wealth and ensure their family is taken care of in the future. The book covers a range of topics, including wills, trusts, estate taxes, asset protection, and more. It is written in an easy-to-understand style and is perfect for anyone who wants to learn about estate planning and take control of their financial future.

Copyright Statement

Copyright © 2023 Jon A. Zahaby, Esq.

All rights reserved. No part of this book may be reproduced, distributed, or transmitted in any form or by any means, including photocopying, recording, or other electronic or mechanical methods, without the prior written permission of the author, except in the case of brief quotations embodied in critical reviews and certain other noncommercial uses permitted by copyright law.

For permissions requests, please contact the author at hawaiitrustattorney@gmail.com

Dedication and Acknowledgment

I would like to acknowledge the author, Martin M. Shenkman, for all of his incredible writings on Estate Planning, Limited Liability Companies and Taxation and the author, Valerie Allen, and *AuthorsforAuthors.com* for encouraging me to write.
Most of all, I dedicate this book to my wife of 20 years, who convinced me to go to my first writer's convention. As always, I am weak, but he makes me strong!

Disclaimer

I do not mean this book to be a substitute for legal, tax, or insurance advice from a professional in your jurisdiction.
   This book provides a light summary of the topics discussed only. There can be no assurances every bit of legal information in this book is current and in force. Laws and regulations change every day and information that may be helpful in a general sense may not be useful for specific situations.
   Carefully review your own matter with an attorney specializing in estate planning, taxation, real estate, and entity formation in your state before proceeding with any transaction. As always, also use your own wits and intelligence to decide the best way to move forward in your own life.

Simple Estate and Asset Planning   Jon A. Zahaby, Esq.

CONTENTS

INTRODUCTION

CHAPTER I
Simple Real Estate Mistakes to Avoid

CHAPTER II
I Have a House, A spouse, and Children Now What?

CHAPTER III
Asset Protection for Real Property Owners

CHAPTER IV
Can My Business Hurt Me and My Family?

CHAPTER V
What is Liability?

CHAPTER VI
But I Have a Two Million Dollar Umbrella Policy

CONCLUSION

INTRODUCTION

My clients have made some mind-boggling decisions throughout my 20-plus years of practicing law in Hawaii. From gifting an expensive piece of real estate to their adult children, who promise to take care of them, to purchasing a home with a new jobless boyfriend, some of my clients' life choices and asset management have astonished me.

These are often well educated clients. Some of the worst culprits at personal asset management are those with high-demand careers that give them little time for monitoring personal affairs. Physicians, engineers, and other lawyers come to mind when I think back to some of the biggest disasters and financially ruinous decisions I had the pleasure of cleaning up.

It is an odd category many exceptional people fit into: "wealthy and educated but naïve." These persons may possess large amounts of money, assets, praise, and accolades but lack experience and time to manage them. This makes them a target and easily misled. I have overly trusting clients as well and this can put them at risk also. I actually had a physician call me to go over the initial terms of his prenuptial agreement while he had me on speakerphone with his fiancée present. He didn't bother to tell me she was listening until halfway through the call. This physician takes in over $1,000,000.00 per year and his fiancée makes only $50,000.00.

Many clients come to my office suffering from what I call the "look what I have disease." The world at large does not need to know about every personal and family asset they possess. As I will explain throughout this book, do not hold out real estate, business, and liquid assets and title those assets in personal names on every occasion. Often, money and assets are much easier to get than they are to keep.

In researching how to best counsel and advise my own clients, I have read dozens of asset management, protection and wealth distribution books written by the most brilliant legal minds of our generation, but these texts are too complex for the average person. A good percentage of these books are too complex for lawyers, unless they are also a Certified Public Account (CPA), and focus too much on personal wealth preservation and deferring or avoiding taxation. Yes, taxation and tax management are important. A properly constructed tax plan can help asset owners and their beneficiaries save significant sums of money and can help a business run smoothly and cost effectively. However, tax planning is of no help if there are no income or assets to tax or if we are making minor mistakes and aren't revealing them to professionals until it is too late. Therefore, taxation is not my focus for the average individual, small business, or family. Instead, I focus on helping people make the most of their assets.

Another problem with most estate and financial planning reads is a tendency to pretend there are wealthy, financially sophisticated people around every corner who are making big moves and need high-level wealth transfer advice. Or they pretend there is a boatload of multi-million-dollar businesses that need succession planning urgently.

My research showed over 90% of US adults are NOT millionaires. We are regular people, working regular jobs or we own little businesses that are barely making it. We are sophisticated in some things and novices at others. Some of my clients are the most amazing artisans, entrepreneurs, medical doctors, first responders and even patent and family lawyers, but they don't know the first thing about protecting their assets. The vast majority of Americans are not geniuses, and our businesses don't gross millions of dollars every year. Although we all opine as if the former is true, I do not mean this information to belittle us. It focuses a professional's attention on the needs of this country and our communities. We are a melting pot of smart, adventurous, hardworking, brave and exceptional people, but it is impossible to have a comprehensive understanding of everything. In fact, I don't want my anesthesiologist to know everything about estate planning or commercial real estate. I would rather they spend their valuable time learning more about anesthesiology and leave the estate planning to me. Professionals who are highly specialized and knowledgeable in specific areas are valuable to our society, and I believe they have an obligation to share information that can assist the masses. It also doesn't do my community any good if I as an attorney focus only on high net worth issues and run around trying to harpoon whales all day. It is more productive to look at the relevant impact on an individual's life that a particular legal decision has made. An avoidable $100,000.00 loss may just be a hiccup to a multi-million-dollar developer, but it can mean the world to the beneficiaries of a small estate.

This book is a compilation of the most often asked questions and recurring themes flowing from my clients during my past 22 years of practicing law in Hawaii. I hope this book will help readers avoid issues that have caused others so much frustration. While I drafted this book from a Hawaii perspective, I believe it can apply to any United States jurisdiction and even internationally. The one thing that makes Hawaii unique, from my practice standpoint, is it has high value residential and commercial real estate but very low-paying jobs for the average citizen. In that respect, the residential home is often the most valuable asset in a family's portfolio. Also, Honolulu is a big city that encompasses both urban and rural areas with some litigious atmosphere added for good measure. Therefore,

Hawaii is the perfect location for showcasing asset protection, estate planning, real estate and insurance issues that can apply broadly to any urban or rural community.

Throughout the book, I have added some sections labeled "Advanced Strategies" or "Sidebars" for further reading on certain tax and asset protection matters. Allow these sections to give you a starting point to research areas that relate to your specific situation. Although these sections are labeled "Advanced", they are only slightly more complex than basic legal planning and worth your time regardless.

One of my hopes for this book is it will be an easy read with simple principles that people with average estates can put into place. However, my biggest hope is it will create a mind shift in my community. We need to look and think critically about our assets and how those material things we have worked so hard for should be maintained and then transferred to our loved ones so they can be used for comfort or help throughout the generations.

CHAPTER I

Simple Real Estate Mistakes to Avoid
Conveying real estate to your children during your lifetime: the inter vivos transfer

I am lying in bed; my head is aching, and I am overwhelmed with anxiety. It is two am and I am not sure why I lay awake. I didn't drink coffee too late. I didn't exercise before bed. I only ate a small amount of food. My mind races, my sheets feel restrictive. Oh, lord. What has my heart so heavy?

Yesterday, yet another client told me they added their child to the title of their house. That's it! The reoccurring nightmare of my practice–and it is horrifying.

Simple Estate and Asset Planning   Jon A. Zahaby, Esq.

The number one mistake that has been threaded through the fabric of my career has been the improper inter vivos transfer. What?

Black's law dictionary defines an inter vivos transfer as:

> "Between the living; from one living person to another. Where property passes by conveyance, the transaction is said to be inter vivos, to distinguish it from a case of succession or devise."
>
> Black's Law Dictionary, 2nd Ed.

More simply, this means signing a deed that transfers all or a portion of your house to your child or children while you are still alive. This is a HUGE mistake. There are many ramifications of this simple act; however, in Hawaii and elsewhere it's continually done by parents who, in their kind hearts, think it is a gift that will help their children. Also, usually a clueless financial advisor has told them the transfer will help them qualify for Medicaid or avoid probate or problems when they pass away. Most of these individuals don't even know the difference between

Simple Estate and Asset Planning   Jon A. Zahaby, Esq.

Medicaid and Medicare. I hear clients in my office confuse them all the time, and I will talk about this at length toward the end of my rantings.

Therefore, some parents are making inter vivos transfers of real estate to their children because they believe they need to in order to get simple Medicare Health Insurance, as they are confusing Medicaid and Medicare. As if that were not crazed enough, there seems to be no end to the list of "professionals" who allow this to happen. Countless mortgage brokers, financial advisors, lawyers, escrow officers, and real estate agents allow their clients and customers to make improper inter vivos transfers without ever informing them of the, sometimes irreversible, ramifications.

The most common way this takes place, in my experience is this: parents will go to a friend who works at an escrow and title company and tell them they want to add their child to the title of their home. Nine times out of 10, without question, the escrow officer will order the deed from a real estate attorney they use for all of their document preparation. Most document orders that come from escrow are for purchases of real estate. The attorney receives a document order from an escrow officer to draft the deed. The attorney does not feel there is an attorney-client relationship because it is a basic order coming from the escrow and title company, and the attorney drafts the deed without making a disclaimer about the ramifications of an inter vivos transfer. Voila! Your child in now on title to the house you and your spouse live in.

So, what's the problem?

(i) The client loses the capital gains tax stepped-up basis. Below, I will discuss what the tax "basis" is on real property and how you only receive a step up in basis when you inherit an asset, not when it's transferred to you during the grantor's lifetime.

(ii) We have transferred a valuable asset to someone unable to maintain or manage it. You love your kid, little Brian. He is a fantastic salesperson at Macy's. He is very loveable and kind. However, Brian doesn't know the first thing about home ownership, and he doesn't have any liquid assets he can use to maintain real property. Brian may need to sell the house when you pass away and downsize so he can make ends meet.

(iii) Joint tenants and tenants in common have a right to the entire property and Joint Tenancy is destroyable unilaterally. There is an odd situation when a property is owned and titled as joint tenants with a Right of Survivorship. A joint tenant can sever the joint tenancy without the consent of the other joint tenant(s) by unilateral act. That act can be by conveyance to self or others. This removes the right of survivorship because the transfer automatically reclassified the interest as tenants in common, which, of course, goes to probate and will eventually convey to the severing tenant's heirs or beneficiaries and not to the former joint tenant survivor.

(iv) Tenants in common have a right to the whole property as well. Many people want to break down the ownership interests in real property in terms of percentages, so they choose tenants in common. What they don't realize is each tenant in common alone has rights to occupy, use,

15

profit from, and possess the entire property. This is true even if the percentages of interests are unequal. You gift your niece Betty a 1% interest in your vacation home so she can handle some things to do with the property (get a parking key card) when she stays there on vacation. Betty moves in 24/7 – 365. Now what? What are your rights to the property that you own 99% of now? Answer: The same as Betty's.

(v) Divesting assets rarely works for Medicaid Planning. We will discuss this further later in this book, but it's important to note improper divestiture of assets for the sole purpose of qualifying for Medicaid can result in a Medicaid back lien being placed on your personal residence in order to recoup monies paid for your care by the government. However, one thing nobody ever thinks about when they're all jazzed up on Medicaid planning is how truly dismal and unfavorable Medicaid long-term care facilities are. A great sales tactic for financial advisors looking to sell long-term care insurance products would be to have a photo album of some of these places. As part of our law firm and service to the community, we offer mobile notary services for all of our documents. This service takes my wife and I on to the campuses of many Medicaid-funded facilities, such as nursing homes and hospice. They are not places I would want my loved ones staying in for an extended period. Please talk to your insurance advisor about long-term care or even short-term care insurance products.

SIDEBAR: what is the difference between Medicaid and Medicare?

As we've been discussing, clients often confuse the two programs that mostly concern the elderly and/or disabled: Medicaid and Medicare. While they are both government insurance programs, they are very different.

Medicaid and Medicare are both birthed from the Social Security Act of 1965. Medicaid is designed for indigent individuals and Medicare is public health insurance for Americans 65 or older and others receiving Social Security Disability Insurance (SSDI). Medicaid has federal rules governing its implementation, but it is conducted and partially funded by each state separately. This means Medicaid program (Medquest in Hawaii) qualifications and processes can differ across states. Medicare is federally managed and funded, so it is the same in every state.

The big differences between the two programs are how one qualifies and what they cover. In very simple terms, if you paid taxes for a decade and are 65 or older or you are receiving SSDI, you qualify for Medicare. Other than a waiting period, that is about it. You will need to pay for your Medicare Plan so it can be helpful to discuss your options with a Medicare plan specialist. Now, qualifying for Medicaid is a whole different, annoying ball game. As it should be because, again, it is for low-income individuals. This is a point often lost on clients who wish to qualify for the program but own a multi-million-dollar house.

Generally, if your income and assets fall below a certain threshold, you were a foster child, you collect SSDI, you are "medically needy" or you have certain types of cancer, you can qualify for Medicaid.

The key takeaway for estate planning and asset protection is Medicaid can fund long-term care and Medicare cannot. However, Medicare can cover hospice and short-term care. Also, as discussed, Medicare has other plans you can add and costs money while, generally, Medicaid is free until you pass away, and liens can attach to your assets to pay back Uncle Sam.

Capital Gains Tax

Capital gains tax is tax due upon the profit realized from the sale of a fixed asset. This most commonly occurs when real property, stocks and bonds are sold. The capital gains tax problem created by an inter vivos transfer from parent to child is the child will receive a carryover basis rather than a stepped-up basis.

The Internal Revenue Code §1014 provides the basis of certain assets will be adjusted at death to the fair market value at the date of death of the decedent. In most situations, the basis of an asset is what it cost you.

I won't bore you with more of the tax details but in very simple terms if the real property (real estate) is inherited, meaning the grantor is passed away when the grantee receives the inheritance as opposed to the asset being gifted during the grantor's lifetime (inter vivos), the grantee will receive a step up in basis to fair market value usually at the time of grantor's death.

The difference in receiving a step up in basis rather than carrying over the original basis of the grantor can mean massive differences in amounts of money subject to capital gains tax when the grantee sells the real property. This is also a capital gains problem in many "old style" A/B trusts. If you see your parents or others have old A/B trusts drafted years ago, suggest a review and amendment because their trusts could include (bypass trust) provisions that will cost beneficiaries taxes.

You purchased your house in Pearl City, Hawaii for $125,000 in 1975. It is now worth $1,250,000. You were talking to a real estate agent about adding your child to the property since they are living there anyway, and you don't want them to have to go to Probate Court when you pass.

Also, your Financial Advisor said you might need to qualify for Medicaid, and you can't own any assets. (By the way, all poor advice and, generally, untrue.)

So, you add your child to the house by deed, either the entire interest, joint tenant or tenant in common, and they now have a tax basis of $125,000. If your child sells the land for $1,250,000, they will then have a taxable gain of $1,125,000 ($1,250,000 sales proceeds minus $125,000 basis).

If, instead, you kept the land and transferred it to your child at your death (by using a revocable living trust) when the house is worth $1,250,000, your child would have a tax basis of $1,250,000. If they sell the land for $1,250,000 then they would have no taxable gain ($1,250,000 sales proceeds minus $1,250,000 basis).

While the calculation may be different if adding your child to the title as a joint tenant or a tenant in common, the general idea is the same. Instead of conveying the entire interest in real property to their children, many clients believe placing children on the title along with themselves is a good idea and a great probate avoidance strategy.

This is a horrible idea. Many people add their children to the title of real property as joint tenants with a right of survivorship because upon the death of one joint tenant the interest of the deceased automatically transfers to the other joint tenant without probate court involvement.

This creates the same capital gains problem we have already discussed, but with even more complex math because it also involves a gift tax return filing requirement by the Internal Revenue Service (IRS): IRS Form 709.

I can't remember a single client, other than CPAs working with estate planning clients, who has ever heard of Form 709. No one knows about it and nobody, other than my wealthiest clients, complies with gift tax filing requirements. There is an annual and a lifetime gift tax exclusion; less than $20,000.00 for the annual exclusion as I write this book (May 1, 2023).

Therefore, you are technically required to file a Form 709 when you convey a title to your child because the value of the real property conveyed is over the annual exclusion. While you may not owe any taxes because you can borrow from your lifetime exclusion, you still have the obligation to file Form 709.

Another unforeseen problem with joint tenancy is unilateral transfer can destroy joint tenancy by one joint tenant acting alone and without the consent of the other joint tenants. If one joint tenant conveys, by quitclaim deed, their interest in the real property without telling the other joint tenant then the other joint tenant will have their interest automatically converted into a tenant in common interest with a percentage ownership shared with the new tenant in common owner.

Note each tenant in common has full rights to the entire house, no matter what their percentage of ownership. Say goodbye to your private bedroom. All tenant in common interests in real property go to probate court when the tenant in common title holder dies because there is no right of survivorship like with joint tenancy.

I have seen this happen hundreds of times when lay persons take real property transfers into their own hands. There are so many disputes between co-tenants of real property because deeds are so easily recorded with no one knowing the ramifications of the transfer and with no co-tenancy agreement between tenants in common or joint tenants which dictates how the parties will share, manage, and maintain the property.

Advanced Strategies

Capital gains in estate planning: loss of stepped-up basis for second spouse in old fashioned A/B and QTIP trusts

President Biden actually proposed ending the step up in basis at death. The government would have nothing to do if we all just agreed we have enough laws. I digress. It is best to "keep it simple, stupid" with planning. Unless you are dealing with a business succession of the wealthiest of clients with third marriages and crypto currency, the simplicity of marital deduction planning with a revocable living trust that is flexible is unmatched.

With a revocable living trust you can give the surviving spouse the choice to:

    a) elect portability of the deceased spouse's unused exclusion;

    b) disclaim into a credit shelter or bypass trust; or

c) both.

   d) You can also move beneficiary interests into Dynasty trusts to avoid disputes between siblings.

That way you don't lose step up in basis via a strict, cold and old bypass trust.

More Advanced Stepped-up basis versus Carry-over Basis

This comparison mostly involves whether beneficiaries who sell an inherited, appreciated asset will pay capital gains tax on the gains from the time of the asset's original purchase (plus some mumbo jumbo CPA stuff) regarding cost of any improvements less depreciation equals the basis or carry-over basis or from the time that of the asset's inheritance or the stepped up basis. For more information about the Internal Revenue Code, Section 1014, see 26 U.S. Code §1014. This is where much of income tax planning for estates is taking place now that the estate tax exclusions are very high.

Simple Estate and Asset Planning   Jon A. Zahaby, Esq.

Vesting during purchase of real property

"But Jonny, I don't have the deed to the house; the bank has the deed!"

"Don't worry, I will pull the document for you, but just so you know, the bank does not have title to your house. The bank has a mortgage recorded on the title to your house. There is a big difference. The deed is in your name."

True story: once a week, a client with a home worth over one million dollars has the above conversation with me. Many people do not know what happened during the escrow and purchase of their real property. They believe they will not receive the deed to their houses until they pay off all mortgages encumbering the property in full. To us, in the industry, it seems insane you would put 20% down on a HUGE ticket item in cash, pay property taxes twice a year, property maintenance, work in your yard, put in solar panels, and have absolutely no idea who is on title to the property. At least 75% of clients I've come into contact with do not know where the deed to their house is located.

Would you purchase a $120,000 automobile and have no idea where the title is located or who is on it? Something is falling through the cracks with realtors, title and escrow officers. Even if escrow and the real estate agent have kept their clients informed and educated, many still do not know HOW or in what manner they hold title.

SIDEBAR: Escrow Agents and Realtors

Escrow is a neutral third party that holds funds and documents during a real estate transaction. Its role in a property purchase is to ensure both the buyer and seller fulfill their obligations in the agreement, before releasing the funds and transferring ownership of the property. Escrow officers do not offer legal advice. The escrow officer must remain unbiased because they are an intermediary only.

Then on the other side of the coin is your realtor. Let's not mince words: real estate agents and brokers are not qualified to give legal advice. Legal advice is best had from a licensed real estate attorney. Realtors may have a general understanding of real estate law (two days a week for six whole weeks of basic classes), but we should not rely on them for legal advice.

Back to our regularly scheduled program–as to holding title as tenants in common, during the escrow process, the title company will send the buyer a questionnaire, usually titled "Vesting," asking the buyer how they wish to hold title. The form usually has check boxes for tenants by the entirety, tenants in common, and joint tenants.

The title company and their attorney will probably not offer any advice on how to hold the title. Unknowing buyers will check off tenants in common because they don't really comprehend the meaning, they come from a community property state, or they knowingly wish to hold title by percentages which only tenants in common ownership offers.

Possibly one owner contributed more than the other toward the purchase of the real estate. However, as we touched on above, there are several negatives that flow from tenants in common ownership. Tenants in common interest do not avoid probate court.

If one tenant in common owner dies and we do not hold the interest in trust or there is not a transfer on death deed, the tenant in common interest will need to go through the probate court process and a personal representative must accept appointment before it is possible to transfer the property to the deceased's heirs. Logically following, no right of survivorship exists for the other tenants in common that owned the real estate with the deceased.

The deceased tenant in common owner's interest will not go automatically to the other real property owners, as with joint tenancy and tenants by the entirety. Each tenant in common owner's interest will distribute to their heirs at law or to those beneficiaries designated in each tenant in common's last will and testament.

This is an often nasty result for longtime unmarried couples that just assume they will receive their significant other's interest in the house they live in when their partner passes away. There have been many occasions where a grieving girlfriend of 30 years has sat in my office not able to comprehend how she is now forced to sell the home she has lived her life in, paid for maintenance and improvements, cleaned and cared for because her deceased boyfriend's children are now on title to her home.

Yes, many unknowingly become title holders with the adult children of their deceased boyfriend or girlfriend during their advanced years. Rarely are the adult children from a previous marriage compassionate in this situation.

Married couples are also surprised when the vesting form comes from escrow. It has surprised me to find a document order from a title company in my email inbox ordering me to draft a deed for married individuals as joint tenants with a right of survivorship.

Nobody bothered to advise them that in a tenants by the entirety jurisdiction, married couples may hold title in that form of title. Presently, there are about 26 states that have tenants by the entirety in the books. In jurisdictions that allow title to be vested as tenants by the entirety, it will always be a vastly superior form of real property ownership over joint tenancy.

The magic behind tenants by the entirety harkens back to the days of English common law. They considered a husband and wife to be one and therefore when they received property, they received it in a "unity of interest" that is not destroyable, unlike tenancies in common and joint tenancies.

In practical terms, it means one spouse's liability alone cannot attach to the real property held as tenants by the entirety. This applies to judgment creditors as well. I cannot record a judgment from a court of law against one spouse alone on the title of real property held as tenants by the entirety. In this litigious world, one would be hard-pressed to find an asset protection strategy that is more powerful and more easily and cheaply implemented than simply accepting title by deed as tenants by the entirety rather than joint tenants.

Therefore, it is my opinion when drafting joint tenant deeds for clients and escrow officers it is blatant malpractice not to disclose to married couples the advantages of tenants by the entirety and give them a warning about the form of title they are about to encumber their property with.

We can glean a few things from these examples:

i) never take advice from anyone that took a six-week course to start their profession; and

ii) work directly with an attorney that specializes in property and asset transfers if you wish to transfer property during your lifetime.

Therefore, you know a professional has properly apprised you of all issues. Notice I said, "work directly" because when title companies and mortgage brokers retain attorneys to draft deeds for their customers, those attorneys rarely advise the clients they are about to make an estate, asset protection, probate, or tax mistake.

They do this because they consider themselves merely scribes or drafters of your and your title companies wishes. These attorneys are 'retained' for the very narrow scope of drafting the deed and the escrow company is usually recording the document. So, of course, they will not list for you every ramification of making the transfer.

Due-on-Sale Clauses

An additional matter deed drafters will not address when they draft a deed ordered from an escrow officer is the acceleration of loans caused by transfer of real property encumbered by mortgages. Almost all commercial mortgages have a due-on-sale clause drafted into the document which gives the lender the power to call the full amount of the loan due at once should the mortgagor make an improper transfer of an interest in the encumbered real property without authorization from the lender.

A due-on-sale clause is a provision in a mortgage contract that requires the borrower to repay the entire mortgage balance in full if they transfer ownership of the property to any person or entity not allowed under that clause. This means the borrower cannot sell and transfer the property to a grantee, transferee or buyer without giving the lender the right to demand immediate full repayment of the loan.

However, the due-on-sale clause or acceleration provisions cover more than transfers during the sale of the property. Most due-on-sale clauses also prohibit transfers to irrevocable trusts, LLCs, and corporations. The due-on-sale provision protects lender's security interest in the property and ensures the mortgagee receives payment on the loan. In practice, many more sophisticated real estate investors regularly violate the due-on-sale clause because they feel the benefits of re-titling real property in the name of an LLC for liability purposes outweighs the risk of loan acceleration.

So long as the loan payments are being made, exercising due-on-sale clauses by lenders is extremely rare on loans that are not in default. Would you violate the due-on-sale terms of your mortgage and give your lender fodder should you later experience payment issues?

Holding Title to Real Property as Tenant in Severalty

Yet another common mistake I have witnessed is unmarried individuals that buy a house and the escrow company, realtor, and everyone else involved automatically assumes and encourages the unmarried buyer to hold the title to their new property as tenant in severalty (as a single owner in their own name). This is especially dangerous when the property is an investment or rental property. I have dealt with countless clients that owned free and clear real estate in their own names. I call this naked and flying solo. Remember, young'un's, homeowner's insurance doesn't cover intentional acts.

The reasons I dislike tenant in severalty are:
    i.   if you pass away the real property will go to probate and;
    ii. if you damage or injure someone and they obtain a judgment against you, the house is attachable by judgment, exposed and possibly lost to the judgment creditor.

This is one of the most fully exposed big-ticket items most single individuals possess. I can't stand ownership of real property as tenants in severalty. A more prudent move is to convey the real property to a limited liability company (LLC) or a trust-owned LLC in order to separate the asset from their personal name or other business that they run. I will talk much more at length about limited liability companies later in this book.

So, as you may now realize, the seemingly innocuous vesting form that is sent from your escrow officer when you purchase a residential or investment property can have far-reaching ramifications depending on how you answer the form. In fact, I have spent much of my career and legal life informing clients about how an insignificant event or decision can flow into disaster or success.

People, real estate agents, investment advisors, and entrepreneurs are supposed to be optimistic, and someone trained them to be hopeful. Alternatively, they train attorneys to look for the worst-case scenario. While this mentality is not good for the attorney's mental health, it is greatly beneficial for clients.

Always seek the advice of a knowledgeable attorney to review your escrow documents and purchase contract as most real estate agents, escrow officers, and mortgage brokers are not qualified to advise you to regard all aspects of real property ownership, nor should they be.

Look at each individual helping you through any process regarding your assets, marriage, education, or health and think about what their principal job or purpose is. The mortgage broker's main job is to get you a loan. The real estate broker's primary job is to find you a buyer or find you a home. In the healthcare arena, we have all heard of preventative health care. In the legal context, the attorney's job is preventative asset protection.

Life Estate

A grantor can deed real property to their children or other beneficiaries and "retain a life estate" on the same real property. This establishes two types of real property owners: the life tenant and the remaindermen.

With a life estate, the grantor retains the exclusive right to live on and in, use, rent, and profit from the real estate while they are alive. I've used life estates for years to help my clients avoid probate and protect their real property from Medicaid back liens. I could write another book on the Medicaid back lien but in a nutshell, although the Federal Government pretends it is, Medicaid is not free.

Medicaid or MedQuest will place a lien on your personal residence even though it is not a countable asset for qualification for Medicaid assistance. The lien is for the government to recoup Medicaid monies spent on the deceased's care before we can convey their residence to heirs.

Before Medicaid planning trusts existed, the life estate was the only viable strategy to preserve my clients' largest asset and maximize tax benefits for their beneficiaries as well. Maximization of tax benefits occurs if and when the beneficiaries sell the real property because they receive a stepped-up basis when the life tenant passes away.

They nicely avoided probate because the remaindermen automatically take ownership upon the death of the life tenant with no probate court intervention. Note this is not a strategy for anyone that does not absolutely trust their beneficiaries because it is a strategy that uses an irrevocable conveyance (i.e., the life tenant cannot sell the property without remaindermen's consent unless all parties involved agree otherwise).

CHAPTER II

I Have a House, a Spouse and Children–Now What?

For the vast majority of American citizens, planning an estate and organizing assets is to ensure one's possessions easily flow to heirs or beneficiaries pursuant to their wishes. We all want to avoid conflicts between our beneficiaries and help them circumvent a lengthy probate court process or even a battle in probate court. We worked hard to acquire our assets and we don't want them eaten away by litigation and disorganization when we pass away. It is a rare occasion for the average small-town lawyer to come across an individual or couple with a large enough estate to necessitate complex income tax or estate and gift tax planning trust work. Therefore, I focus this chapter on probate avoidance and revocable trust planning. Let's not bore ourselves to death with irrevocable or tax planning trusts, with all of their acronyms, *Irrevocable Life Insurance Life Insurance Trust* (ILITs), *Spousal Lifetime Access Trusts* (SLATs), and *Intentionally Defective Grantor Trusts* (IDGTs), until those vehicles are absolutely necessary for your situation.

What is this "Probate" We Are Always Trying to Avoid?

Unofficially, well, it is annoying, even for attorneys, and expensive in even the most organized courts in the United States. It is a complete nightmare in courts where organization and funding are a challenge. Often the probate court staff are either overwhelmed, unhelpful, or on a power trip because they have been doing the same job under flickering neon lights for 25 years.

Simple Estate and Asset Planning   Jon A. Zahaby, Esq.

Officially, probate is a court process where a court administrator or a judge reviews the assets of a deceased person, identifies inheritors, heirs and/or beneficiaries and assists distributing those assets to the proper people. Most people do not understand probate is multi-generational. This means even if you or someone else on title received the property via a probate, your heirs must probate it again when you pass away.

I just recently ran into this issue when a personal representative's deed placed multiple family members on title to a home here in Honolulu. I had drafted an estate plan for the couple that paid for the previous probate and now they wanted to convey their interest in the home to their trust. The problem was the home had these other family members on title. I had to instruct them that unless each family member on title also placed their interest in a trust or filed a transfer on death deed, they would embroil their beneficiaries in another probate each time one of the other family members on title passed away. This is even though they did the right thing and avoided probate of their interest for their own children.

The probate court can use the deceased's last will and testament as instructions for distribution of the estate assets or if there is no will the probate court will distribute the assets pursuant to that jurisdiction's rules of succession reflected in the state statutes. Usually, a state's statues are a form of the Uniform Probate Code.

Like almost all court proceedings, a probate petition is a public matter, so anyone that might wish to contest a distribution or any creditor that may have a claim against the deceased's estate may enter into the probate proceeding and file claims or grievances.

I have witnessed an unusually exorbitant amount of greedy remote family members snooping around every time there is a probate in Hawaii. The stretches in logic some people will go to convince themselves they are entitled to something from a deceased distant relative will cause one to question their faith in humanity.

For all the above reasons and more, most probate petitioners or personal representatives must hire a probate attorney to help them with the process. Probate legal fees and court costs can be astronomical if there is a dispute during the process. Contention, complexities and time that a probate case entails can be an enormous strain on already grieving family members.

Luckily, almost all probate cases are avoidable by the use of revocable trusts, transfer on death deeds, joint tenancy, and tenancy by the entirety.

How to Resolve Disputes With Siblings and Relatives In and Out of Probate

Even if you've been extra careful, paid all the legal fees and set up a stellar estate planning strategy for your family, your siblings and other relatives may have done absolutely no planning or may be ignorant of the necessity for estate planning.

At least once per week, I have a discussion with someone that has a family squabble regarding an inheritance or jointly held property. This happens so frequently when parents leave a piece of real estate to multiple children as beneficiaries; it leads me to think as estate-law practitioners we need to devise a logical strategy for disclosing the pitfalls of joint ownership between siblings to grantors.

These repeated, costly emotional and financial battles are wholly unnecessary and often driven because grantors appoint the wrong persons as their representatives. If they are adults, I will ask to meet the beneficiaries. Sometimes after meeting them, I suggest the grantors use a non-family member as trustee or personal representative.

So, what do we do when we share inherited assets with siblings or other relatives, and we end up in probate? How do we resolve issues with estranged or difficult family members?

Often problems rear their ugly heads when one party believes the person grantor(s) appointed as trustee or personal representative is not fulfilling their obligations to the other beneficiaries or trying to shift ownership of joint assets to themselves. Unfortunately, the latter is often true. The best advice I can offer to clients is to make all efforts to resolve disputes outside of probate court. Once a family turns its power over to the courts and attorneys, they are going to pay down part of the estate in fees and still end up with the same mutually acceptable agreement you could have obtained via a family meeting or a more formal mediation.

Simple Estate and Asset Planning   Jon A. Zahaby, Esq.

Are there provisions or other documents that we as estate attorneys can provide to clients in order to make things go more smoothly? The sibling dispute problem is so prevalent in my jurisdiction that I've started offering co-tenancy agreements and/or dynasty trusts for grantors with beneficiaries over 18 years of age to sign in situations where real property is being left to more than one sibling. In other words, "sign an agreement with your brothers and sisters that dictates how you will share ownership, manage, maintain, and sustain the real property that we as grantors are leaving to you or do not take under the trust.

It is especially useful for siblings that turn into greed monsters the moment their elderly parent becomes incapacitated and attempt to sequester that parent from the rest of the family. This happens very often. One sibling granted with a durable power of attorney will attempt to exercise undue influence on a parent to amend, change, or revoke the revocable documents that an estate attorney has drafted in order to cut their siblings out or bolster their inheritance share.

Attorneys are not psychiatrists and while they may have a battery of questions for incompetency when the notary shows up, they may not have enough contact with a grantor, or may not care enough, to ensure the parent/grantor is not being unduly influenced by a greedy or substance addicted child.

That is why agreements between siblings regarding real property that they will inherit are helpful to deter the propensity for greed or misunderstanding. At the very least, grantors should have their estate attorney explain the no-contest provisions in their trust to their beneficiaries and the ramifications of wasting the assets of the trust on attorneys and court fees by falling into dispute.

Another strategy often used by estate attorneys is to ask parents/grantors to draft a letter of instruction to their children. We must be very careful with this strategy because that letter must absolutely NOT conflict with the distribution language in the trust or will.

However, if the letter of instruction written in layperson's terms parallels the distribution in the trust, it can be very helpful for helping the beneficiaries, and even the probate court, to understand what the grantor's wishes were.

Not to judge, and I don't know everyone's reasons for doing things, but leaving uneven distributions to a few siblings is a HUGE mistake and almost never ends well. If you don't want a portion of your estate to go to attorneys and the court system when you die, don't leave uneven distributions without discussing your reasoning with your beneficiaries at length.

Simple Estate Planning

Okay, I don't want the problems you're pointing out, but what is an estate plan and why do I need one?

Many misconceptions about trust and will planning come from the idea of the "trust fund baby" sitting on a pile of cash from wealthy parents. Yes, wealthy people need estate planning and if you are or become lucky enough to build wealth, you will need to modify your simple estate plan to allow for more advanced techniques if you want to save your beneficiaries' taxes and headaches.

However, every adult needs a simple estate plan. This usually includes at the very least (and not favored by me) a last will and testament where you let the judge know who you want to distribute your assets when you die and who you want those assets to go to.

Also, every adult needs to ask themselves if they need to think about what would happen if they became incapacitated or otherwise unable to manage their own affairs. As most of us know, incapacity and disability are not afflictions that are limited to the elderly. We can answer these questions through the drafting process of a power of attorney.

When I talk about simple estate planning, I am not talking about tax planning for high-net-worth individuals. They probably will not read this book, and I am okay with that; they have attorneys, CPAs, brokers, and financial advisors. Simple estate planning is for individuals that might have any of the following: a house they live in; a rental property; a vacation property; children; a few cars; a life insurance policy; 401K; and an IRA. That includes all the people out there pretending they have more. Don't go into shock. I read the intake sheets.

Regular people care about avoiding probate, designating heirs and beneficiaries, reducing taxation, getting taken care of when they are elderly or incapacitated and caring for children and grandchildren. A comprehensive estate plan can address all concerns above.

A good estate plan includes a revocable living trust, pour-over will, power of attorney, advanced health care directive or living will and some other ancillary documents and letters for personal property and burial wishes.

In Hawaii and some other states, the last few are statutory forms, so they are pretty uniform: the statutory powers of attorney under Hawaii Revised Statutes §551E and the advanced health care directive under Hawaii Revised Statutes §327E. There are many similar statutes and legislation across the country. So, with little effort, you can avoid subjecting your family to conservatorship and guardianship proceedings in court.

Powers of Attorney

There are three basic types of powers of attorney:
   i) limited powers of attorney–where you authorize someone to act on your behalf for a limited purpose

and/or time period, such as signing on a purchase agreement;

ii) springing powers of attorney – where the powers only "spring" alive when you are incapable of managing your own affairs, as determined by one or two physicians; and

iii) general durable powers of attorney–where the powers granted to your attorney-in-fact are immediately in force upon execution.

For most married couples, attorneys use general durable powers of attorney so a spouse can immediately manage the other spouse's person and property should they become incapacitated. Some parents appoint children as their power of attorney wish to use springing powers because they don't want to risk mismanagement of assets or give up control assets unless a physician designates them as incapacitated.

This is often inconvenient for representatives of the family because doctors are famously non-responsive to requests for letters of incompetence. This is because the declaration of someone as incapable of managing their own affairs comes with liability for the doctor.

Advanced Health Care Directives or Living Wills

Living wills are usually standard documents in which you appoint health care agents who will act on your behalf. You can also express your wishes regarding your organs, end-of-life decisions, and living arrangements. Doctors and nurses will usually ask you if you have these documents.

Remarkably, this is the document most of my clients anguish about. Many hardly bat an eye at the revocable trust that dictates where all of their material belongings will go, but they toss and turn about whether to donate organs, have artificial feeding or pain medications at the end of their lives.

Sibling Co-tenancy Agreements

In a perfect world, siblings that own real property jointly can come to an agreement on the use, sale, management, and maintenance of the real property they inherited. We don't live in a perfect world, unfortunately. So, as discussed above, co-tenancy agreements outline and dictate certain terms beneficiaries must follow if they to jointly own inherited real property.

For example:

(i) how the beneficiaries can use the property as a co-tenant or joint owner;

(ii) when and how the real property must be sold; and

(iii) if they do not sell the real property, will there be a buy-out or right of first refusal? Sometimes a trust will talk about the sale of a certain asset, but in reality, they seldom account for these terms in the distribution provisions of a revocable living trust unless a dynasty trust for beneficiaries is included. Just like the requirement for letters of instruction, we need to make sure the sibling co-tenancy agreement jives with the language in the trust.

Letters of Instruction

The letters of instruction document is where you can put in plain language what your wishes are as a grantor. You can explain complex estate planning terms to your loved ones, and you can also explain to your successor trustees how to disperse assets that may only have sentimental value.

Grantor(s) can also say things in this letter that may be too emotional or hurtful to place in a trust that banks or other institutions may see. A good letter of instruction does not conflict with the terms of the trust and may include:

- a list of all assets, including personal items and the location of those assets;
- all account numbers and bank and investment details.;
- location of all keys and codes for any property, crypto vaults, safes or safe deposit boxes;
- preferred charities; and
- locations of all important documents of importance.

Estate, Gift and Generation-Skipping Taxes

The focus of this book is on regular people and not on high net worth individuals. At the time I am writing this book, the exemptions for the above taxes are so high they are not much of a concern for regular people.

However, a summary is helpful. We are presently under the Tax Cuts and Jobs Act of 2017 (TCJA). The federal exclusion for estate tax is over 12 million dollars adjusted for inflation as time goes by. For example, the exclusion for 2023 is over 12.6 million dollars. So, you (as an individual) can generally leave that amount to your beneficiaries on the same level or one generation down and pay no estate tax and need no fancy estate tax planning.

Some jurisdictions, such as Hawaii, decoupled from the federal exclusion and may have a lower exclusion, so you need to talk to your tax advisor or estate planning attorney in your resident state if you're blessed enough to have at least half of the above exclusions in assets. The TCJA will sunset on January 1, 2026. Sunset in estate planning language means estate planners have absolutely no idea what congress will do about estate, gift and GST taxes after that. Educated guesses are just guesses.

Revocable Living Trusts.
What is a Revocable Living Trust?

A revocable living trust is a changeable (revocable) trust document in which a grantor designates beneficiaries of their assets, such as real property, personal property, cash, stocks, bonds and other worldly possessions, both tangible and intangible.

Revocable living trusts are used to avoid probate, enhance privacy, and protect beneficiaries from creditors and unsavory persons. Revocable living trusts are important tools for both individuals and married couples. The typical estate plan involves an estate planning attorney conveying an individual or couple's real property to the name of a revocable living trust(s) and assisting them to set up bank accounts in the name of the trust.

This is called 'funding' the trust. Note there are many "trust mills" or online legal document providers that will never tell you that you need to title all assets you want to pass to your loved ones via the trust in the trust's name. Once we properly titled assets in the name of the revocable living trust, the initial trustees, which are usually the same persons as the grantors, manage the asset just as they did before we created the trust.

The assets that are titled in the name of the new trust will pass to the beneficiaries named in the trust with no probate or any government involvement other than obligatory tax filings. As a bonus, a well drafted revocable living trust will contain more complex provisions that are used for tax planning and beneficiary asset protection. If there is a sizable estate, or one spouse is a foreign citizen, a custom trust can be drafted to accommodate the most tax efficient and smooth transfer of assets.

While I am well versed in marital deduction planning, disclaimer planning and QTIP provisions, and I will touch on them all below, they are beyond the intended scope of this book because I wrote this book for laypersons, and it is a foolish lay person who drafts their own trust taxation provisions.

Because the marital deduction planning splits the estate into several buckets, it creates a nightmare for the successor trustee(s), risks income and other tax mistakes and we should not use it lightly.

Other provisions that are very helpful in revocable living trusts which make them a preferable vehicle, as opposed to joint tenancy or transfer on death deeds, for instance, are spendthrift or substance abuse provisions.

It is much more difficult for a creditor of a beneficiary to deal with a trustee that has the power to withhold funds or assets from a beneficiary than a drug addicted beneficiary that has just received a valuable asset via an outright distribution.

While joint tenancy and transfer on death deeds do work to avoid probate, their distribution of assets is automatic and outright. This might expose the assets to creditors and "friends" of the beneficiary.

What is a Transfer on Death Deed?

At the time of writing this book, about 30 states authorize transfer on death deeds or lady bird deeds. A transfer on death deed is very much the same as any deed a grantor would execute to transfer real property to someone.

However, the difference is with the transfer on death deed, the transfer does not take place until the grantor passes away. More and more states are adopting the Uniform Real Property Transfer on Death Act (URPTODA), which authorizes this type of death transfer deed.

However, for some of the above reasons I've covered, I don't favor this type of estate planning. If a comprehensive estate plan is not in a family budget it just is not, so, for less complex estate planning and wishes, it is an acceptable option for passing real property and preferred over having only a simple will and going to probate.

Remember, however, transfer on death deeds have none of the asset protection value I have described when I talked about tenants by the entirety and revocable living trusts having limited asset protection value.

Also, if you change your mind about beneficiaries, revocation of transfer on death deeds with your state or county recording office is a clumsy process. The last place you want your intended beneficiaries to be is in a squabble about what document they recorded when at the filing and recording office of your state or county.

Revocable living trusts are "King" because unlike all other probate avoidance tools, tenants by the entirety, joint tenancy and transfer on death deeds, revocable living trusts cover probate avoidance on the second spouse or beneficiary to die and not just the first to pass.

As we discussed, the trustee of a revocable living trust can also withhold assets from a beneficiary that is experiencing creditor or substance abuse problems. Remember the tenants by the entirety ownership of real property can often be carried over to the trust for added asset protection, depending on the situs of the trust. These trust provisions and comprehensive estate planning documents can go a long way to protect familial wealth and that is why trusts are the preferred method of wealth transfer for well-advised clients.

I caution any wills-only planning. It is possible to do joint tenancy with right of survivorship, transfer on death deeds and wills-only planning (with testamentary trust provisions) that will avoid probate, but in my experience these plans are sloppy, confusing, and invite the government and recording office into your life to approve your documents and potentially invite people to contest your wishes after you are gone.

More Advanced Tax Planning Strategies

The Internal Revenue Code has three types of taxes for estate transfers:

    (i)   Chapter 11 of the Internal Revenue Code, Section 2001: the estate tax for transfers at death;

    (ii)   Chapter 12 of the Internal Revenue Code, Section 2501: the gift tax on lifetime transfers; and

    (iii)   Chapter 13 of the Internal Revenue Code, Section 2601: the generation skipping on transfers to individuals two or more generations below the grantor.

These taxes, the filing requirements and how your attorney or CPA can avoid them are important to at least be aware of for the average layperson. Although the exclusions are very high on a federal level, they may be lower in your state as we've already described that they are lower in Hawaii.

Simple Estate Tax Planning for Wealthier Married Couples

The Internal Revenue Code allows a deduction from the decedent's gross estate for property in a qualifying marital deduction trust for the benefit of a surviving spouse. The marital deduction is unlimited in amount. By leaving all of one's property to the surviving spouse's marital deduction trust, an individual may ensure the individual's estate won't be subject to federal estate tax if their spouse survives them.

Now there are a myriad of different formulas attorneys and CPAs use in order not to "overuse" the marital deduction. However, for this book, I want you to at least be aware of the marital deduction. If you are coming up against the exclusion amount as your estate grows, you want to know you can use the marital deduction effectively both via a trust and otherwise.

Simple Estate and Asset Planning   Jon A. Zahaby, Esq.

    I don't want to lose anyone, but please also, talk to your attorney and CPA about "portability" if you amass a sizable estate and need to use the unused portion of your deceased spouse's exclusion amount. At the time of writing, May 1, 2023, Hawaii allows portability on the state level as well. A disclaimer trust is a similar vehicle that can be used, so please ask your professionals what will work best for your situation.

Gifting and Playing with the Gift Tax Exclusion

Internal Revenue Code, Section 2503(b) allows each individual to gift, to any donee and however many different donees, a certain amount annually (for 2023 it is $17,000.00) adjusted for inflation incurring no gift tax and with no gift tax filing requirements.

    Attorneys and CPAs use this to reduce the size of an estate during the lifetimes of wealthy clients so when they pass away, there will be a less sizable estate, hopefully under that year's exclusion amounts.

Of course, there are brilliant techniques to put limitations on these "gifts" so we are not just spending and spoiling kids all over the place just to avoid estate taxes. However, don't be a turkey and give your gift exclusion amounts during the holidays if you can afford it. In my experience, parents don't mind gifting money or assets to their children during their lifetimes. They just don't want them to actually enjoy wealth while they are still young! I jest.

However, many of my clients feel exactly this way when I bring up gifting as a way of avoiding estate and gift taxes. The topic is always a hard sell. It opens your eyes to the fact there are often many non-tax concerns that trump tax concerns. Especially when those tax concerns are going to take place after an individual has passed.

I will not discuss generation-skipping taxes in this book. If you are a wealthy client or you have wealthy clients who are beyond exclusions and skipping generations, you may wish to reexamine your estate plan and structure more complex trusts with generation skipping or dynasty sub-trusts.

Even after the exclusion amounts sunset in 2026, the "smart" wealth transfer crowd roughly estimated the exclusion for each individual to be around $7 million. Since most people in the United States will not be concerned with estate taxes, income tax planning has become all the rage.

Therefore, my ultimate word on estates and taxes is to watch out for and ask for planning that gives you and your family the full use of the step up in basis at both the first and second spouse to pass away.

Please focus on emotional and liability non-tax issues on your estate planning journey. Saving an irresponsible spouse or child estate or capital gains tax means nothing if we haven't been honest with ourselves about that person's ability to manage the fruits of our labor.

Irrevocable Trusts

Irrevocable trusts are where estate planning complexity really ramps up. It is the most complex area of law. Irrevocable trusts are used to transfer assets to protect the assets funded into the trust and providing for beneficiaries.

The scary thing about irrevocable trust is the irrevocability of them. The grantor gives up control and ownership over the assets they place in the trust. I commonly used these trusts for estate planning and tax reduction for wealthy individuals.

Like limited liability companies, irrevocable trusts can protect assets from creditors, provide for family members with special needs as I will describe below, and manage assets for minors or other beneficiaries who cannot manage their own affairs.

We all have to be extremely careful with these trusts because it is very difficult to undo transfers, and the tax mistakes can be severe. Some modern legal ideas, such as decanting, can undo some (but never all) of irrevocable trust provisions once they are in place. Unless tax savings are significant or asset protection worries great, these trusts are sometimes not worth the risks. However, they are fun to manipulate and discuss with other lawyers.

Special Needs, Supplemental Needs and Medicaid Trust Planning

Approximately, one in six children in the United States has a disability. Many adults also have an accident or develop some kind of disability during their lifetimes. I see people every day live exceptional lives while also dealing with a disability.

Therefore, although this book is not about all of the different types of complex trusts and planning we do on a daily basis, it warrants a brief discussion so we can also protect the assets of disabled persons in our families.

A special needs trust is a type of trust created to provide health, financial and educational support for a person with disabilities, while preserving eligibility for government benefits such as Medicaid and Supplemental Security Disability Income (SSDI).

The funds in the trust can be used to pay for a restricted list of expenses, such as medical care, education, housing, and personal items, without affecting the beneficiary's qualification for government benefits. Family members or a court often establish these trusts for the benefit of someone who cannot manage their own finances. There are two main types of special or supplemental needs trusts:

- (i) A first-party special needs trust is established using the assets of the person with special needs. The first-party special needs trust is subject to Medicaid back lien provisions, which require the state to be reimbursed from the trust assets for benefits provided to the disabled person by Medicaid or Medquest; and
- (ii) A third-party special needs trust is established using assets belonging to someone other than the person with special or supplemental needs. The difference between the two is the origin of the assets that will fund the special or supplemental needs trusts. A third-party special or supplemental needs trust is not subject to Medicaid back lien provisions.

As you can see, it is very important if you have a family member that has a disability which would qualify them for SSDI or other governmental benefits that family members do not gift or devise to that family member outright. This is because a gift or devise could disqualify them from benefits. It is also important to establish these special needs or supplemental needs trusts before the individual with special or supplemental needs gains assets. This is sometimes unavoidable because the very accident that caused the disability may also be the accident that awards the individual a settlement.

Therefore, a savvy plaintiff's attorney that avoids trial and enters into a settlement agreement with the defense attorney can dictate in that stipulated settlement where the judgment award monies fund (i.e., a special needs trust versus the person in their individual capacity).

Medicaid trust planning is very similar to special needs and supplemental needs planning. However, it is typically for elderly individuals that expect to need Medicaid to foot the bill for a nursing home or in home nursing care. Using a special type of trust, called a Medicaid trust, we estate-planning attorneys can preserve assets for individuals with long-term care needs while still allowing them to be eligible for Medicaid benefits.

The purpose of establishing the Medicaid trust is to ensure the elderly individual's assets are used to provide for their care without affecting their eligibility for government assistance programs, like Medicaid and Medquest. The Medicaid trust also avoids the Medicaid back lien. The following is a common scenario that comes up in my practice often.

Robert is 83 years old and maintaining his health on his own is getting very burdensome. So, he goes to a Medicaid advisor because he wants to apply for Medicaid long-term care assistance he heard about from his cousin. Robert bought a house in Honolulu for $30,000.00 in 1973 and it is now worth $850,000.00. However, the Medicaid advisor tells Robert not to worry because his primary residence is a "non-countable" asset for Medicaid qualification.

Unfortunately, this is only half the story, and it is the most common version of the story. Yes, Medicaid will not count Robert's house as an asset when he applies for Medicaid but when Robert dies, they are going to put a lien on Robert's house for all the money they paid on Robert's behalf toward his long-term and any other care. At $8000 to $12000 per month for long-term care, even $820,000.00 in equity can be eaten up pretty quickly. I often see the home a grantor thought they were giving to their children sold to pay off Medicaid back liens.

CHAPTER III

Asset Protection for Real Property Owners

Will this lawyer ever stop talking about tenants by the entirety? No. In some jurisdictions, as mentioned above, a married couple can hold the title as tenants by the entirety.

The well-settled law, since the time of common law, is only penetrable by the Internal Revenue Service and the Child Support Enforcement Agency. Many couples don't even know how they hold title and often assume it is joint or "something" and feel no need to check because they are "together" as a unit. So, tenancy by the entirety or separate ownership gives us protection against the creditors of only one spouse. However, what happens when both spouses are on the hook for some judgment or damages? Homeowner's insurance or an umbrella policy? Most people talk about insurance as if they have experience tendering a claim. It is not as cut and dry as most people think. Believe it or not, insurance companies are not in business to pay claims.

Remember when Mr. Incredible got fired for paying out too many claims at his insurance job, so he had to go back to being a superhero? If they were looking to pay every claim that came across their desks, they wouldn't be in business very long. Therefore, in order to make full efforts in protecting all family members and assets, some more manipulation of risk is necessary.

I have always adhered to the basket theory of asset ownership. Never keep all of your possessions in one basket for all the world to access, know about, and enjoy. By carefully arranging the family estate in different baskets, we can achieve this objective.

For example, small businesses should operate as separate entities, usually owned by limited liability companies. Include vacation and rental properties in the small business category, as they should often be owned by separate limited liability companies as well.

In the construction world, we call these LLCs special purpose entities and we borrow this idea from construction projects. A big construction project is never done under one umbrella. Different entities (LLCs and Corporations) are created to undertake different phases of construction. We can apply this to small businesses and personal holdings as well. The separate basket method of ownership will reduce the bleed through from misfortunate occurrences that may happen involving one or more persons or assets within the family.

I had a client call me at 8am on a Saturday–let's call him Kawika. Kawika owned several rental properties in Honolulu his father left him when he passed away. However, Kawika was not the savvy real estate investor and agent his father was. He was a very talented auto mechanic. Unfortunately, a severe injury took place at the shop he worked at and they rushed one of the employees to the hospital. Forty-eight hours later, the injured party was dead.

Simple Estate and Asset Planning   Jon A. Zahaby, Esq.

The injured party's family sued Kawika. He was underinsured, and the court also found him to be grossly negligent in his maintenance of the shop equipment. The court handed down a judgment against Kawika and the award far exceeded both his insurance and personal assets. In order to satisfy their judgment, the plaintiff's attorney sought to attach Kawika's rental properties that he naively held in his own name as tenant in severalty. After hundreds of thousands of dollars in legal fees, Kawika lost the shop to the plaintiff along with his father's properties.

Now before you jump to judge Kawika for his faults and lax business behavior, examine your own life and work performance. When was the last time you lost your temper or became so angry you wanted to hurt someone? When was the last time you made a huge mistake driving that, luckily, did not end in an accident? When was the last time you imbibed a few too many libations or drove after consuming legal marijuana? When was the last time you had a relationship that did not work out?

We are human beings with faults, emotions, and even mental illnesses. We are living in a litigious, cancel culture that does not tolerate mistakes. This should give you motivation to carve your livelihood away from your personal assets immediately.

Bank Accounts

Most people, including lawyers, are not aware a married couple can hold a bank account as tenants by the entirety, just as they hold their real property. The principle can apply to liquid assets. A bank account can be held at an investment firm as tenants by the entirety.

However, you must always request this form of ownership from your financial advisor. The investment firm or bank will never automatically place your bank account in tenants by the entirety. This omission is a breach of fiduciary duty in states where tenants by the entirety are available, yet you never hear of a bank in hot water over the omission and general lack of concern for their customers. Make sure you formally request your banker or investment banker titles all of your existing joint accounts as tenants by the entirety if you are married and have it available to you in your state.

Another way to protect assets in bank accounts from creditors is by setting up a trust or a limited liability company and transferring your bank account into it. If the trust is structured correctly, it can protect your assets from creditors.

This method usually involves the use of irrevocable trusts and limited liability companies that are established in jurisdictions that afford members of entities creditor protections such as charging order protection, which restricts the rights of creditors to collect distributions from the business.

You must be very well informed when establishing these trusts and entities and titling a bank account accordingly because not all states are created equal when it comes to protecting their citizens from creditors. Some states are so bad at protecting your assets they will let any clown with a spurious claim freeze your bank account or enter your safe deposit account.

LLC Owned Real Estate

If you are holding rental properties in your portfolio, creating a limited liability company is a straightforward decision. Deed the property out of your personal name and into a limited liability company to shield your other assets from what might or might not happen on the property. Caveat emptor applies, however. There are potential negative side effects of conveying your property to a limited liability company and several twists and turns many people go down in the process that create a real mess.

Make sure your property is a rental or investment property and not your personal residence. Not only make sure of this in your own eyes, but in the eyes of your mortgage company, the state, and the municipality that governs your homestead or real property tax exemption.

You need to go back and examine your mortgage or refinance documents closely to determine if a due-on-sale or acceleration clause prevents you from conveying the property to an LLC. The potential penalties for a transfer prohibited by these clauses can be devastating.

Simple Estate and Asset Planning   Jon A. Zahaby, Esq.

An acceleration clause is just what it sounds like: if you make a prohibited transfer, the loan accelerates and becomes immediately due and payable. Ouch! Many provisions in residential real estate mortgages prevent such a conveyance and many lenders have restrictions on transferring interests in the mortgage documents. Do not assume because you previously transferred the property to a revocable living trust, you're allowed to make the same type of transfer to a limited liability company.

Fannie Mae and Freddie Mac have made carve outs in residential loans, allowing encumbered interests in property to be conveyed to properly drafted revocable living trusts. However, they still disallow transfers to entities and irrevocable trusts.

Also, check to see if your county or state will allow your homestead exemption if you convey your property to a limited liability company. Most will not–you must do a cost-benefit analysis. Taxation versus exemption. Residential Loan versus investment property loan.

Even with these terrifying warnings, in the twenty-plus years I have been practicing real estate and business law, I have never witnessed a loan accelerate or a mortgage company exercise the due-on-sale clause in a mortgage because of a prohibited transfer. I have had a lender instruct my client to immediately transfer the interest back to the client's personal name, but that was the most severe case.

In the business chapters later in this book, I will give you instructions on how to properly create and maintain a limited liability company. That chapter will also apply to your rental real estate holdings titled in a limited liability company.

Simple Estate and Asset Planning   Jon A. Zahaby, Esq.

CHAPTER IV

Can My Business Hurt Me and My Family?

~ ~ ~

Sole Proprietorships

Another amazing issue in this day and age is many business owners run their businesses as sole proprietorships. A sole proprietorship is a business run by one person who has no legal distinction from its owner. The massive exposure to liability that a business owner subjects themselves to may outweigh the advantage of simplicity and tax structures.

    I am sure if you are this far along in the book, you can name the multiple issues and matters that can go horribly wrong with business and personal assets titled in the same name. Following is a reenactment of a phone call

Simple Estate and Asset Planning   Jon A. Zahaby, Esq.

I once received late on a Friday night of a holiday weekend.

Mr. Client:

Jonny, I tried to access my account to take out some cash for the long weekend and the bank informed me my accounts were frozen. I can't access any of my accounts.

Me:

The best you can do is try to get into court next week.

Mr. Client:

But I have a big birthday weekend planned for my wife's 50th birthday at the X named Fancy Hotel.

Me:

Crickets.

No, I am not some heartless animal; I understand. However, I had warned this client and the other partners in his company to take the separation of business and personal assets seriously. They always said they would, but people often ignore good advice or their lives become too busy.

I even advise clients in high-liability careers or businesses that are often scrutinized by taxing authorities to not only separate their personal and business assets immediately but also to keep cash in a safe. Imagine the implications of showing up to your bank where you hold your life's savings and finding out a plaintiff's attorney has convinced a judge to freeze your accounts, and your bank you have been banking with for 35 years happily went along with the order with no objection.

I see you standing there like an imp with your business banker and no access to any funds at all. No money in a separate entity's business account, no money in a tenants by the entirety or joint account, no money in a protected account where SSI payments also go into, no money in an *Employee Retirement Income Security Act* ERISA (federal asset protections) protected account, no money in your pocket, no money in a drawer or a safe. No money!

Simple Estate and Asset Planning   Jon A. Zahaby, Esq.

I sympathize because I've seen it happen. A judge can let a litigation movant and their attorney into your bank account and even into your safe deposit box. The IRS can freeze your account and wait for you to prove to them you don't owe them money. Don't be a naïve!

In the case for which the narrative above loosely belongs, the client was a partner in a construction business that took out a $100,000.00 loan and defaulted on it. The lender's attorney sued and got a judgment against all guarantors on the loan because the client never received service and did not show up to defend himself in the litigation.

The lender's attorney, experienced with this type of case, also had a home field advantage in the Hawaii courts. Icing on the cake, the lender's attorney was able to freeze all guarantors' bank accounts. With no quashing, counterclaims, cross-claims, or objections, the banks happily complied with the freezing of the accounts. The banks you trust to protect your money will not be there for you when the pinecone hits the fan. Trust me, if I handed them a court order, everyone would comply. The defendants had less than zero negotiating power to settle.

All of this trouble and the clients' limited negotiating power resulted from the operation of businesses as a sole proprietorship and/or partnerships where liability has no limits. The partners also commingled their personal and business assets, making it even more of a breeze to shut the guarantors completely down.

Setting up multiple businesses and accounts titled in different ways is not just asset protection attorney mumbo jumbo. You may thank the gods for having access to a corporate credit card or irrevocable trust account if your financial life doesn't always go your way.

How to Create and Maintain a Proper Limited Liability Company

"But I filed the articles of organization with the state!"

Famous last words.

Countless business and rental property owners have filled out my firm's estate planning intake sheet and listed a limited liability company as one of their assets. When I dig deeper, I often discover what small business owners and rental property owners assumed was a properly created limited liability company was a mere shell of a company.

This brings me to the concept of "piercing the corporate veil"–a phrase that is often thrown around by attorneys to make themselves appear experienced in business law litigation, but what does it really mean and what are the real-world mechanics that bring this about?

Take this scenario: another business or person damaged, either financially or physically, by an employee or member of a limited liability company. The owner of the defendant's limited liability company was a savvy businessman. He didn't need a high-priced attorney to help him set up his business.

He went online to his state's secretary of state or commercial affairs office and filled out the online form for articles of organization for a limited liability company. Fifty dollar filing fee and Bam! Approved. He didn't check off the section that stated the members would not be liable for the debts of the company, he didn't put himself as manager of the company in order to shield the members from the world, and he didn't add any partners to bolster the strength of the corporate structure. Nah.

No need–especially devastating was this business owner never drafted, or hired an attorney to draft, an operating agreement because he either didn't know about it or mistakenly assumed the articles of organization and operating agreement were the same document. Even more dangerous is the company, its member(s) or shareholder(s), and employees are running around town firmly believing they operate as a corporate entity with all the bells, whistles and liability protection such entities afford their owners.

Ah, not so savvy, but these are real-world examples from my experiences. In fact, many small business owners that had otherwise good intentions by filing with the state in the first place are in the same position as this court defendant someday. So, why is this so bad?

Most states have case law and statutory provisions that will allow the court to pierce the corporate veil and set aside the otherwise 'limited' liability of the company in order to hold the members or shareholders of that company personally liable for the company's actions or debts. While the requirements that each judge must follow vary depending on jurisdiction and previous cases, there are three main common elements that will get the judge convinced to blow up your limited liability company:

(i) the company is merely an alter ego of the member(s) or shareholder(s);

(ii) there is a unity of interest or excessive commingling between the company and the member(s) or shareholder(s); and

(iii) the sole purpose of the entity is a sham or fraud, and playing along with the fiction would be unjust.

Triggering these or similar elements will allow the plaintiff to attach personal assets owned by the member(s) or shareholder(s) in order to satisfy judgments and debts against the company. In simpler terms, not acting like a company can cause a third-party adjudicator to ignore the existence of that company. Commingling assets, not having separate accounts or mixing personal and corporate accounts and funds, and not having company meetings, minutes, documents, and records can make a company very susceptible to piercing the corporate veil.

Real companies have quarterly meetings of the board of directors, members or shareholders. A real company has corporate accounts. Real companies have a way to purchase shares or membership interests and charging order protections for their members. A real company has insurance. All draws, salaries and loans to and from a smoothly running limited liability company become properly documented by the LLC secretary and valued.

Proper business and entity structure is extremely important. Not only is having an operating agreement important, but not having some $49 piece of rubbish from an online "LLC" website is even more important. The business owner will never know the documents and how they have their business structured are major failures until it is too late. Properly drafted operating agreements and shareholders' agreements contain provisions that make it very difficult and unattractive for a plaintiff to become a member, transferee, assignee, or shareholder.

Follow me for a second: if a judge grants a plaintiff a membership or shareholder interest, does that plaintiff want immediate tax responsibilities, liability, and capital contribution requirements? This goes beyond mere lay person chit chat about companies, but limiting and/or maximizing new member, shareholder or transferee rights and requirements are incredibly valuable tools attorneys much wiser than I have developed.

I would say there is a high chance of cheap, online shareholder operating agreement forms containing none of these complex asset protection provisions. Don't even get me started about jurisdiction and charging orders, but remember the terms. Also, remember just because the law is not well-settled in your jurisdiction doesn't mean you can't put those clauses into your operating agreement anyway.

I hear so many otherwise-intelligent attorneys spew off case law and omit important asset protection language because they don't feel it would be foolproof and may not always hold up in court. I put it in anyway. You never know what the person in the black muumuu (the Judge) will do and what kind of stamina your adversary has to deal with all of your document language.

If you live to the typical life span, you will probably be a defendant in a lawsuit at least once in your lifetime. An attorney experienced in asset protection can give the small business owner a proper assessment of the business structure and whether it has any holes where piercing the corporate veil or liability can seep in.

Many such attorneys will also be familiar with the idea of forum shopping and which state has the most corporate friendly legislation for your organization. All jurisdictions have somewhat different statutory provisions that govern entities.

For example, Wyoming, Nevada, South Dakota, Alaska and Florida all have some aspects of their laws that are favorable to companies and their owners regarding liability or tax savings. Seeking an attorney well versed in these states and the distinct advantages and disadvantages each offer can make real-life differences for your business and your family.

As with choices of agreement provisions and creation jurisdictions, there are also different ways you can choose to have your entity taxed on both the state and federal levels. For example, they can tax a limited liability company as a disregarded entity (sole proprietorship), an S-Chapter corporation, or a partnership, depending on the circumstance.

Therefore, it behooves small business owners to talk to a good tax professional with experience in taxation of corporate entities. A CPA or tax attorney can give small business owners direction on the structure and operation of the business in the most tax-advantageous way. Also, cueing in your business creation attorney to the conversation will be helpful because sometimes liability avoidance and tax advice can conflict, and the two professionals can find a common ground where they both feel comfortable with your level of protection.

Remember, the IRS is a creditor as well. The company's needs will probably change as the business grows. That is why limited liability companies have been more and more favored. You can start a limited liability company taxed as a sole proprietorship and later file to be taxed as an S-Chapter corporation as you gain revenue and employees. These subjects should be a topic of discussion at the company's annual and quarterly meetings. That way, you kill two birds with one stone. Avoiding alter ego status and making sure the company is performing at its best.

As we all witnessed during the COVID-19 pandemic, everything can change overnight. The way a business was operating one year may not pencil out in a subsequent year. A cost benefit analysis is a good idea to assess the value of CPA and legal fees against tax and cost savings.

S-Chapter and C-Chapter Corporations

What is an S-corp and How is it Different From an LLC?

Much like the limited liability company we have discussed, an S-Chapter corporation is an entity that passes its taxable income through to the underlying shareholders. Subchapter S of the Internal Revenue Code breathes life into this entity and it is meant to only be available to small businesses with fewer than 100 shareholders. I call S-corps LLCs with Aloha shirts on.

While this is not a tax-focused book, S-corps can lower shareholder's personal taxes by defining payouts from the company as salary income or dividends. S-corp shareholders can also be categorized as employees, which opens the door to many healthcare and insurance products and planning. However, I urge caution. S-corps have wide discretionary powers designed for when and how they pay shareholders with dividends. I feel S-corporations are a much higher audit risk than LLCs because of the self-employment tax/dividend issue. S-corp formation documents and shareholder agreements are more complex than LLC formation and operating agreements. Often CPAs will elect S-Chapter taxation without letting the attorney know and the operating agreement is never amended to comply with S-corp requirements. With complexity comes risk for non-compliance and dispute.

S-Corps Verses LLCs

Both entities are pass-through entities for taxation. However, LLCs are much less complex and more flexible because they are not restricted to shareholder and ownership limitations of S-corps. As mentioned before, S-corps are a bit more complex in formation and maintenance and a bit more expensive as maintaining them correctly is difficult without the help of a CPA.

S-corps have much more access to funding if growth is on your horizon.

My suggestion is, when in doubt, start with an LLC and either make an election to be taxed as a S-corp or change to an S-corp structure if the growth of the business warrants it. A word of caution, however, if you're advised by your CPA to make an S-corp election using IRS Form 2553, your job is not done! You will need an attorney to do a complete overhaul of the LLC's operating agreement, if that amendment is even possible. So, I am not a fan of this election. I much prefer for an S-corp to be properly formed as a corporation and not as some puzzled-together LLC Frankenstein.

S-Corps Versus C-Corps
"The taxman commeth."
Murder She Wrote, Season 7, Episode 15

C-corps are taxed by the IRS at the corporate level, and S-corps are not. The need for a C-corp is in a realm outside of the population targeted by this book. However, if you plan to have over 100 shareholders or you are sure you will go public with a stock offering (IPO) soon, a C-corp is for you.

    Generally, S-corporations and C-corporations are taxed differently in the United States. S-corporations (and LLCs) are pass-through entities, meaning the business itself is not taxed on its income. Instead, the income, deductions, and any credits of the S-corporation flow through to the individual shareholders and are reported on their personal tax returns. Shareholders pay taxes on their share of the company's income at their individual tax rates.

    C-corporations are taxed as separate entities. They pay corporate income tax on their taxable income and the IRS also taxes any dividends that are distributed to shareholders as personal income to the shareholders. This results in a "double taxation" of the profits, as they taxed the profits at the corporate level and then again when profits get distributed to shareholders as dividends or income.

ADVANCED STRATEGIES

Tax Classification Choices

Disregarded entity/sole proprietorship: income, losses, and credits reported directly by the owner are subject to tax at the owner level.

Sole proprietorships have no tax issues at the entity level because the business owner conducted business in the owner's name and social security number without creating any limited liability company. You or your CPA will report taxes on the calendar year. No separate return needs to be filed, and the business owner reports everything on your Form 1040 and accompanying schedules. Remember, there is no liability protection at all.

Partnership/pass-through entities: income, losses and credits pass through to the owners or members and are subject to tax at the owner or member level, whether actually distributed.

General partnerships, limited liability partnerships, limited liability companies, and S-Chapter corporations are all pass-through entities (PTEs). Note that general partnerships have no liability protection. There is no entity-level tax on the income of PTEs unless the state where it is operating has established a separate PTE taxing scheme. An LLC is almost always the entity of choice for clients with small businesses, and Form 1065 and Schedule K-1 is how to pass through income to individual partners or members appears.

S-Chapter corporations: all shareholders must file IRS Form 2553.

I find S-corps overly restrictive for almost all situations that my clients foresee within their respective businesses. Even though there is no corporate-level tax, and the income passes through to the shareholders the same as with limited partnerships and limited liability companies, they have other attributes that make them unfavorable. S-corporations may have only a single class of stock, whereas a limited liability company, for example, could have different membership types.

Also, S-Chapter corporations cannot have other legal entities as corporate shareholders. So, doubling up on the liability and asset protection barriers is more difficult. No more than 100 shareholders and no foreign shareholders for S-Chapter corporations also make this structure unattractive for clients.

C-Chapter corporation: subject to income tax at the corporate level and then subsequently at the owner or shareholder level if income or dividends distribute to the owner or shareholder.

The problem with willy-nilly creating a C-corporation when you are starting a new business is that once you pull the trigger, going back could be a taxable event. You almost never need a C-corporation unless you will go public or selling to venture capitalists.

Double taxation is also a colossal risk, especially if you have investors. These entities were all the rage when the Tax Cuts and Jobs Act (TCJA) introduced a 21% corporate tax rate. However, I guarantee there were some very disgruntled clients that found out the tax advantages did not pencil out as promised and could not unwind their structures without tax issues.

Taxation of Pass-Through Entities

Most small businesses in the United States are not taxed at the corporate level. The typical LLC or S-corp profits flow through to members or shareholders and are taxed under the individual income tax. Pass-through entities (PTE) include, but are not limited to, the LLCs and S-corps I've been pushing on you to protect your assets.

In response to the growth in use of these PTEs, the legislature has placed limits on deductions that business owners can take for state and local taxes (SALT). They reflected this in changes to 26 U.S. Code, Section 164, also known as the Tax Cuts and Jobs Act. Several states (not Hawaii) have implemented some version of PTE taxation at the corporate level in order to ease effects of capping deductions.

For specific amounts and how it works, talk to your CPA, but the thing I want you to take away from this is there are ways to use multiple trusts (sophisticated trusts such as Nevada and Wyoming Incomplete Non-Grantor Trusts), charitable contributions and jurisdiction shopping to help your PTE business with the burdens of taxation at the state and federal levels.

Business Succession Planning

If after weighing out the pros and cons of selling or passing on the business with value over the exclusion amounts you decide to pass on the business, you will want to pass as much of the business as possible to your heirs.

The enormous exclusions make it easier to use traditional estate planning methods to transfer assets of the family business to the younger generations. If the value of the business is greater than your estate tax/gift tax exclusion for the year you wish to retire, be sure to discuss with your business attorney whether they're well versed in wealth transfer taxation.

Some methods used these days are intentionally defective grantor trusts, non-grantor trusts, SLATs, GRATs, dynasty trusts, and gifting and installment contracts.

Note: There is a difference in the valuation of a business for transfer among family members from the valuation of the business for sale to a stranger. Knowing the discount and what the IRS will see as reasonable are important.

Along with estate tax planning, you will need help with income tax planning, depending on the value of the business. Therefore, charitable giving and charitable trusts may come into play.

CHAPTER V
What is Liability?

Liability is when you are legally responsible for something. In the context of this conversation, that "something" is "damages." It is a dirty word, I know. Individual human beings or companies can damage other people, things they own, businesses they run and other companies. When damage happens, the damaged party wants to be made whole.

However, they have limited options to search for material remuneration or specific performance to make them whole. They must look to the wrongdoer's insurance, their own insurance, the courts, or all of the above.

So, of course, we all go out and buy insurance when we open a business. For example, general liability and professional liability, and we purchase additional riders to cover what we consider important. However, what happens when we tender a claim, and it becomes a fight with the insurance company? What happens when there is an intentional act? What happens when there is gross negligence? Meaning you or your employee acted in such a blatantly wanton way it is almost as if you did it intentionally. What happens when you want to counter claim for your own damages as opposed to just defending yourself? What happens in horrible tragedies that go above insurance limits? These examples live in the gray area where having properly organized assets will give you a leg up on defending yourself or your company and negotiating power in litigation.

I want to throw out an unfortunate word: "superficiality." Being disingenuous and "on the surface" with the general public is the standard corporate technique for avoiding liability. Once real people connect on a deeper personal level, liability rears its ugly head.

Simple Estate and Asset Planning   Jon A. Zahaby, Esq.

When Harold Homeowner deals with Gary the Garage Door Installer instead of Garage Doors LLC, things get messy. When Tessie the Tenant is renting a room and writing checks to Aunty Lani Landlord instead of Ohana Lani Homes LLC, things can get personal. Relationships are a high liability when money exchanges. Not only do accidents happen, but people have remarkably diverse expectations regarding outcomes and fairness.

> *The whole problem with the world I see is that fools and fanatics are always so sure of themselves and wiser people are so full of doubt.* --- Bertrand Russell

I would add fools and fanatics always seem to find a like-minded attorney to represent them. I've witnessed many otherwise reasonable couples that are totally okay with an amicable divorce get so trumped up by their attorneys it creates devastating financial and emotional loss on both sides. A reasonable expectation for one person may seem utterly insane to another.

Many rational persons expect when you drive in a parking lot, you go slower than if you were on a freeway. However, we have all seen people who do not agree. Mistakes happen between people sharing a roadway and we do not always meet each other's expectations. Nobody is wholly wise nor wholly foolish. We are human. We get mad. We make mistakes. We blame. We fail.

If one party suffers damages, they are going to look to the party they feel is at fault to make them whole. So, controlling liability is about limiting access to the assets the sufferer of damages at your hand, mistake or intentional, has. Being properly insured and organizing your personal and business assets so they're protected from the general public will go miles towards avoiding a financially devastating payment for your own mistakes and the mistakes of others.

Again, Don't Keep All of Your Eggs in One Basket

In the asset protection arena, we borrow this piece of advice from our stockbroker and financial advisor friends. However, our meaning is more literal than theirs. When

Simple Estate and Asset Planning   Jon A. Zahaby, Esq.

your broker tells you not to "keep all your eggs in one basket" they mean don't take all of your cash and invest it in one stock. If that stock goes down, your entire life's savings goes down. Diversifying our assets is not a new theme. For our personal residences, rental properties, bank accounts, investment accounts, and businesses, we seem to lose sight of that diversification.

Two couples:

1. Jasper and Lani hold all of their accounts, real estate, and investments in their personal names. Their primary residence is held as joint tenants with right of survivorship. All of their money is in a joint bank account. They got their mortgage from the same bank. Their cousin is a financial advisor and they have a joint account at his brokerage. They own their cars jointly. Jasper operates a woodworking business as a sole proprietor. He is usually the only one in the shop, so he doesn't have a general liability policy.

2. Maka and Dianne hold their cash accounts at Morgan Stanley as tenants by the entirety. They also have a cash account in the name of their revocable

living trust that also has tenants by the entirety protection. The house they live in is in the trust's name. They lease their cars and write off the lease on their business. Dianne has a busy bakery that operates as Cutie Cakes LLC. She writes off her phone, internet, car, groceries, and everything else remotely connected to the bakery business. The bakery has done so well they purchased a rental condo in Colorado. That rental condo is owned by Ski Freaks LLC, a Wyoming limited liability company. The statutory agent in Wyoming won't even reveal to the general public who owns Ski Freaks LLC without a subpoena.

As we reach the end of this book, which couple do you want to be when the fudgesicle hits the fan? If you put all of your eggs in one basket and somebody sues you, liens you, and holds you accountable for their damages, they will break all of your eggs, including the ones you need to eat in order to survive the storm.

Just as I was finishing this book, I had a client email me about a tax debt that reared its ugly head after being off the radar for almost a decade. You could feel the frantic

Simple Estate and Asset Planning   Jon A. Zahaby, Esq.

vibes through Gmail. He wanted a referral for a tax attorney in Honolulu. He had very poor advice awhile back and was illegally vacation renting property in Hawaii. He wasn't paying the hotel tax, Transient Accommodation Tax (TAT). Some very unsavory people advised him that everybody vacation rents their places and if you pay the TAT, you will expose yourself as an illegal vacation rental. He was further advised, when he learned of it many years ago by a CPA, that since the business was closed and now defunct, there was no reason to pay the unpaid tax.

    Almost 10 years later, the state taxing authority got right into his bank account and took the money out for themselves. I called a law friend of mine that does tax to see if he could help him and his answer was, "Isn't it too late now, what do you propose?" Uhmm... I am not a BIG LAW income tax attorney–you tell me! If you only have solutions for your clients when times are good and everything is running smoothly, what are you worth? Like a stockbroker that only makes you money when the market is good. Any monkey can do that.

If just one egg breaks in the basket, it will bleed yolk all over the other eggs. That is why we must drill this into our heads and learn to keep our private home, rental properties, and business ventures separated. We should place all unrelated business ventures in a separate limited liability company or S-corp.

For some of my construction company clients, I have gone so far as to use different special purpose entities for different stages of the same project. A separate bank account for a special purpose entity that holds limited funds can go a long way toward protecting personal bank accounts.

Commingling Personal and Business Assets

Business ventures should be in a special purpose entity. We should place even different phases of business ventures in separate entities. When the developer of an apartment building runs a project, they do different phases of that project by unique entities that may or may not have the same shareholders or members. When the project is complete, the developer may retain some rights for a short period, but eventually, they will turn over the entire project to the Association of Apartment Owners and its board of directors. This is to create a barrier, a breaking point where liabilities end and begin.

We may not be this advanced when we are just starting a small business. However, we must be just as cautious about moving money in and out of the business accounts and placing them in our personal account and vice versa. This is one of the key elements a plaintiff's attorney can use to convince a judge to ignore your limited liability company and hold the underlying members liable for damages.

If you take funds out of the LLC account and pay for things that are obviously personal, or pay for business items out of your personal account without reimbursement or inditing the loan, you are commingling business and personal assets. Manage separate accounts for all entities you create, whether they are actively doing business or they are just holding companies for residential real estate or rental properties. Make sure Peters are never robbed to pay Pauls. Allow each entity, including yourself, personally, to run on its own steam. It is always better to operate as a multi-member or multi-shareholder company liability wise.

Most states grant added protections in their statutory scheme for multi-member entities than they do for single member entities. This is because there is a reluctance to allow the fallout of one member or shareholder's life to injure the other members or shareholders of that business.

ADVANCED STRATEGIES

The Realty Trust With Limited Liability Company as the Beneficiary.

I have droned on and on in this book about owning rental property within your very own LLC. I've also bored you to tears with my obsession with tenants by the entirety and revocable living trusts that you carry tenants by the entirety ownership into.

Now, I want to flip the canoe. Ah, wow, I am enthralled. What magic will he come up with now? Don't worry, my friend, I would like to introduce to you the realty trust with LLC as a beneficiary. Go searching around your Secretary of State or your state's Department of Commerce website. For Hawaii, it is the Department of Commerce and Consumer Affairs, Business Registration Branch (DCCA).

Do a business name search and pull up the first name. For example, King Towing LLC. The DCCA or the Secretary of State, in most jurisdictions, cooperates with King Towing's creditors and they will tell you who all the members of the LLC are and where they live. If you use your own address as the registered agent, a plaintiff's attorney can have a ball sending the process server to all the members' houses while they are having a Sunday barbecue. If you use your business address as the member's or manager's address, the sheriff can show up to your business when you have customers and clients around. It should not be the case that a search of your LLC name can reveal so much about you and the distinct assets the LLC (you) owns.

So, if you are looking for more privacy, how's it structured? Some recording offices require revocable living trusts have a title that reflects the full name of the grantor(s) for retention of certain benefits, such as carry over of tenants by the entirety. However, you can forgo those benefits and title your trust with whatever name you wish. A completely anonymous name such as ABC Trust is workable. The trust is an unrecorded trust so nobody, other than the trustee and the grantor, knows who the trustee or beneficiaries are without a subpoena. The distribution of income to the LLC beneficiary should also be under the control, able to be withheld or otherwise limited by the trustee. This is a unique structure that can add privacy while still keeping liability protection.

CHAPTER VI

But I Have a Two Million Dollar Umbrella Policy

As I am writing this, the radio show celebrity, Alex Jones was handed a judgment of one billion dollars. Whaaat? All the craziness he was spewing, I am sure he had huge insurance policies. Not enough, though. HINT: It will never be enough. Remember, insurance companies are not in business because they love to pay claims.

I forgive you for not reading your homeowners or general liability policy (umbrella policy).

They have paid me good money in the past to read several and, even then, admittedly, it was a nightmare every time. I read a J.D. Power statistic that 52% of all homeowners do not understand what their homeowner's policy covers. (J.D. Power 2017 Homeowners Insurance Study www.valuepenguine.com/home-insurance statistics.)

I am more likely to believe 48% of homeowners are lying. Nobody understands the policy. That is the point. What we probably cannot find statistics on is the percentage of claims that are tendered or filed and denied because the policy did not cover what the homeowner thought it did.

Insurance is risk management primarily used to hedge against the risk of a contingent, uncertain loss. There are many insurances, including health insurance, life insurance, car insurance, homeowner's insurance, disability insurance, and long-term care insurance.

Health insurance helps cover the cost of medical expenses, while life insurance provides financial support to loved ones in the event of the policyholder's death. Car insurance provides financial protection in the event of a car accident, and homeowner's insurance helps cover the cost of damages to one's home and personal property.

Disability insurance provides income replacement if the policyholder becomes unable to work because of injury or illness, and long-term care insurance helps cover the cost of long-term care services, such as nursing home care.

Property and Casualty Insurance

This is an all-encompassing term that covers a plethora of different insurance products that protect your home, car, and other assets from loss or damage. Property and casualty can also include injuries you cause to others or damage you cause to the property of others.

While I criticize insurance and how many insurance companies operate, the financial burdens of some incidents would cripple most individuals and their lives without the existence of insurance. Therefore, it is a necessary evil in the same way manipulating ownership of your assets to avoid liability is also necessary. Some common types of property and casualty Insurances are homeowner's, auto, renter's, commercial, landlord, umbrella and even boat, power sports and extreme sports. I encourage my clients to work with a reputable P&C insurance agent that has access to a wide variety of products and won't oversell or under insure you.

As described above, none of these insurances cover intentional acts and they excluded a long list of other things from each respective policy. Are your friend's golf clubs she left in your car covered by your policy? Probably not.

Life Insurance

Every day, I encounter an insurance agent, now called "financial advisors," that espouses the benefits of whole life insurance to everyone they meet, whether they asked for the advice or not. If you have reached the point on the wealth scale where you will pay estate taxes, a life insurance product could help pay those taxes. There are a million different variations of life insurance products on the market today, but this book is not about insurance.

A few ways I have found term, universal and whole life insurance helpful in my practice is that some of those products have ERISA protections (federal asset protections) which can really be beneficial for asset protection purposes. A whole life policy can be funded and borrowed from with liability-protected funds.

There are also private banking arrangements, business succession plans, loan plans, over funding and other strategies that sophisticated insurance professionals can utilize to help persons grow tax-deferred, ERISA-protected wealth. Be careful! Many inexperienced agents exist, and this is one area you really need to work with someone that knows what they are doing. Also, many scam artists practice in this field and I see people trapped into high-fee insurance and annuity products all the time. Review your rate of return, fees and tax ramifications carefully!

Simple Estate and Asset Planning Jon A. Zahaby, Esq.

CONCLUSION

I've gone through 'simple' concepts on how to gain, maintain, protect and transfer your hard-earned money and assets. I hope this information will help all of my beloved clients and my community to preserve their assets during their lifetimes and to pass those things on to their children, grandchildren, and other loved ones.

I went over many legal concepts in this book but there are also some commonsense steps we can all take to reduce the chance of negative effects on our families:

    (i)   Document everything: keep records of all transactions, agreements, and communications related to your business, legal, and personal affairs.

(ii) Follow laws and regulations: ignorance is not an exception to the law. Stay informed about laws and regulations in your community and comply with them to minimize your exposure to liability.

(iii) Do not make any promises in writing unless you absolutely intend to keep them.

(iv) Don't give money outright to persons with financial or substance abuse problems; they will always be back for more.

(v) Avoid engaging in high-risk activities that could hurt others.

(vi) Don't take legal advice from family. Consult an attorney if you don't know what your legal obligations or risks of liability are.

As inflation rises and the cost of living goes up, I have a deep desire to see people in our community and in America avoid financial stresses and pitfalls. Staying out of court is not only a financial issue but also a health issue.

Financial stress is a leading cause of divorce and suicide. Family issues have led to suicide as well. The more we can cut down on familial disputes and financial stressors the better. As we have seen, implementing simple legal strategies can alleviate most issues with family and inheritance.

The same goes for our businesses because our businesses and our jobs are our conduits to the outside world and the vehicles by which we often contact people outside our family.

We talked about the liability that takes place every time we have contact with other people. I make mistakes; my clients make mistakes; and you make mistakes. I want to encourage the American dream and that comes from taking risks. However, I want to limit the fallout if and when things do not go as planned.

Please stay connected with me via my email hawaiitrustattorney@gmail.com and look for my future writings. I always want you to know I am proud of you, and I am in your corner! ALOHA.

Simple Estate and Asset Planning   Jon A. Zahaby, Esq.

ABOUT THE AUTHOR

Jon Zahaby is an Estate Planning, Real Estate and Corporate attorney and author from Honolulu, Hawaii, with over 22 years of experience helping local clients manage their assets and affairs.

As a recovering litigation attorney, Jon has been in the courtroom and witnessed many damaging situations that with some knowledge and planning could have been avoided. He also recognized many books and texts on legal issues are too complex and not user friendly. Therefore, in 2023, he decided to write this, his first book, hoping *SIMPLE ESTATE AND ASSET PLANNING: A Guide to Protect Your Family's Future* will help to spare readers and their loved ones unnecessary hassles and legal pitfalls.

Besides writing, Jon is also an actively practicing attorney and has worked with several prominent charitable organizations and families in Hawaii. Jon is passionate about charitable planning, special needs planning and helping local families, and often volunteers his time.

Jon wants you to know a portion of the profits from this book will be donated to charitable organizations that help disabled and special needs children.

When Jon is not writing or working, he enjoys surfing, martial arts, and spending time with his family.

www.ingramcontent.com/pod-product-compliance
Lightning Source LLC
Chambersburg PA
CBHW071517220526
45472CB00003B/1057